Letters to the Misunderstood

& the Hopeless

THE WORLD IS IN YOUR HANDS

Mose Howard III

THIS BOOK IS DEDICATED TO
THOSE WHO LOST THEIR LIVES
TO GANG VIOLENCE & THOSE
WHO ARE STRUGGLING TO FIND
THEIR WAY IN THIS TROUBLED
WORLD. MAY GOD BLESS ALL
OF OUR HEARTS WITH PEACE
AND LOVE!

To order additional copies of this book, contact:

Mose Howard III

313.673.9131

Prolific.Vision.Enterprise@gmail.com

Prolificvisionenterprise.com

Acknowledgements:

First and foremost, I would like to thank God, the creator of the world, for allowing me to have purpose & for allowing me to withstand my worst days. I would like to thank my grandfather, Mose Howard Sr., who is no longer here with us. A man of my own heart. Someone who I will always admire because he never gave up hope when I was lost but instead, he encouraged me to find the light inside myself. I would like to thank my grandmother, Juanita Howard, for always giving me constructive criticism & for her constant prayers over my well-being. I would like to thank my father, Mose Howard Jr., for accepting me to live with him when I was a teenager. Through the time spent with my father I was able to see a man provide for his family day in and day out with no complaints. Without being able to live with my father in my teenage years, I may not have had the chance to make it to this point in my life. I also would like to thank my mother, Renita Goodman, who has always been in my corner, whether I'm right or wrong. She is the epitome of strength. At a young age I always wanted to make my mother proud because of the unconditional love she showed wholeheartedly to me and my brothers.

Chapter 1: The Introduction

**"The journey of a thousand miles
begins with one step."
-Lao Tsu**

While writing this book 13 people I know have just been indicted on drug & money laundering charges by the FEDS. These are people who I separated myself from because we were going in two different directions in life. Many times, we try to hold on to relationships after they have run their course. That could have easily been my name added to the indictment if I didn't change my environment and the people I associated myself with. Everybody is so worried about being "real" to the next person. Being "real" to someone else could cost you everything so be careful.

So much potential is wasted in prisons and in the cemetery. So many people not caring about themselves & so many people who have no one to care about them. Do you really care about yourself? Do you make decisions that will best benefit you? Or do you put yourself in harms way, making decisions that cause a pattern of losing focus and regrouping.

We all look different, come from different backgrounds & upbringing but we share many similarities dealing with life situations. I wonder how many people reading this book grew up glamorizing someone who had more materialistic things than them and even looking up to that person not knowing what type of things that person had to do to acquire their status or even what type of person they are mentally. I wonder how many people reading this book are still glamorizing someone who has more than them. In simplest terms "The Cambridge dictionary definition of glamorize is to make something better than it is & therefore more attractive." Imagine glamorizing a person's lifestyle whose beliefs are the total opposite of yours. Imagine glamorizing a person's marriage or relationship instead of valuing your own. Imagine glamorizing an athlete instead of manifesting & working hard to be better than the best. Imagine glamorizing someone because they wear expensive clothing or drive nice cars. Imagine glamorizing to be someone that you're not. I am no different from those of you who can relate to this topic. Mislead, misguided & blinded by things money can buy. Following after people who were also blind. It was almost like the blind leading the blind. What's worse is not knowing when you are blind & leading people to destruction.

There is nothing wrong with aspiring to have nice things & a nice life. We shouldn't, however, glorify a person because of their status. Work hard to live out your purpose. Why try to live someone else's life Instead of living the life that's meant for you? We make it so hard to live the life that is meant for us. Have you ever made decisions that are of your own will that led you to a bad situation? I think it's safe to say we all have. Life is all about decisions. Do I go right, or do I go left? Do I listen to instructions that have been given to me by elders or do I find out everything the hard way? Remember our choices have consequences.

Step 4 of the 12-step program is every day a person wakes up they should take a fearless moral inventory of themselves. Do we have to be addicted to alcohol/narcotics to practice steps from the 12-step program? Of course not. Every day we wake up we should take a moral inventory of ourselves. Every day when we look in the mirror, we should be happy with who we are and what we stand for. Every day we wake up we should strive to be a better person and continue to build good character. Every day we wake up we should challenge ourselves to be more productive & not take time for granted. A big regret that people have is thinking they have more time; more time to live; more time to rekindle relationships; more time to rebuild relationships; more time to spend with family; more time to chase your dreams; more time to hold your kids. Tomorrow is not promised so cherish every breath that you take.

"Knowing others is intelligence;
knowing yourself is true wisdom.
Mastering others is strength;
mastering yourself is true power."
- Lao Tzu

To master one's self is a far greater accomplishment than to conquer another person because it takes much more discipline. There was a saying that older people would say to me when I was a young man, it was the first of many contradictions from those who were in a role model position or position of authority. "Do as I say, not as I do." The phrase itself is a contradiction and leads you to believe that children have to follow the rules, but adults can do as they choose.

Why is it so hard to be a good person? First ask yourself what makes a person good. According to **psychologytoday.com** "'Good' means a lack of self-centeredness. It means the ability to empathize with other people, to feel compassion for them, and to put their needs before your own." Good people are not racist, they are able to see beyond the difference of the color of a person's skin or their nationality. Good people do not steal. Good people do not commit malicious crimes towards other people or animals. Good people are not selfish. Good people are compassionate. Good people believe in a power higher than themselves. Being a good person is a choice we must make every day. Strive to be better each day than you were the day before.

As with anything there is always an opposite. If there are good people, there are also evil people. Steve Taylor the author of "The Leap: The Psychology of Spiritual Awakening" defines evil people as those who are unable to empathize with others. As a result, their own needs and desires are of paramount importance. Taylor relates evil people to dictators such as Stalin & Hitler, and to serial killers and rapists. What they all have in common is the inability to empathize with others. Evil people gain pleasure out of hurting other people because they can't sense other people's emotions or sufferings. Evil people steal. Evil people commit malicious crimes towards other people or even animals. Evil people commit selfless acts towards other people. Evil people worship the devil.

The world we live in today is crazy in some countries. It seems that evil people are often praised and glorified. A good person is not perfect. In fact, most people fall in between the lines of being good & evil depending on the circumstances. That reason alone is why so many good people are incarcerated for committing crimes - due to circumstances. Can you blame a single mother who can't find employment or gain assistance that decides to steal to feed her child? What about a man that commits homicide against a man who molested his daughter or raped his wife? Does either of these things make the people evil? Circumstances and decisions can alter a person's life from good to bad in a blink of an eye.

Many youth that get caught up in the street life come from good family backgrounds. Many youths neglect the guidance given to them by their parents and other people that come into their lives because of negative influences. The job of a parent seems to get harder and

9

harder as it becomes normal for children to challenge the authority of those in charge of their well-being. When I was growing up it seemed like all the cool kids were the ones who had the most freedom. Most of the time it was because they failed to listen to the instructions given by their parents and sometimes it was because kids didn't have any parents to give them instruction. Imagine being raised in a home where your guardian is addicted to hard drugs or even abuses alcohol. Imagine being abused verbally and physically. Imagine being molested by someone who is supposed to love and protect you. My heart goes out to the youth and adults who have suffered from a traumatizing childhood.

When I was a child, I witnessed my mother being physically and verbally abused for several years by her husband, who is the father of my two younger brothers. That damaged me and caused me to shutdown emotionally. I didn't know how to express my feelings. I didn't know how to communicate and express my thoughts. I kept all my emotions bottled up and it damaged so many relationships for me while I was growing up. My attitude and my decisions made people treat me unfairly sometimes. Let me explain what I mean by this. Often times people look at a troubled child or youth as someone who needs discipline or someone who needs to find their own way. People gave up on me. I'm not a religious man but I am a spiritual man. One thing I perceive to be true is that God often takes his soldiers through tough battles in order for them to find themselves and find their purpose. I didn't understand my purpose until I stopped going by my own understanding and letting my soul lead me.

It's imperative we stop giving up on kids/youth and start giving them extra love because we don't know what God has in store for them. From growing up being a part of the Crips culture at age 9, to being arrested countless times, to being shot 5 times, to being homeless, to going to prison, I would never think that I would be this motivated. I would never think that I would feel like my past could allow me to help someone else's future. Something has changed inside of me. A light bulb went off and I started feeling like I was worth something. One of the greatest things you can do for someone is pour life into them. I'm 36 years old and for the first time in my life everything is so clear. For me to be who I am, I had to go through the things I did. I'm no different from you. You were created to be exceptional, to stand out, to be great. However, if you don't get out of your own way you will never obtain the accomplishments that are meant for you. There is an African proverb that reads: "When there is no enemy within, the enemy outside can do you no harm." Eliminate all doubts in your mind and eliminate the power that you give other people over your life. Eliminate the people out of your life who do not speak life into you.

Chapter 2: Loyalty

"Loyalty isn't grey.
It's black and white.
You're either loyal completely, or
not loyal at all."

-Sharnay

My brother, William, was given a natural life sentence at the age of 19 for murder. He was convicted after a weeklong trial as he plead not guilty to the charges. William has been incarcerated since 2009 & he is still fighting for his freedom as he continues to find grounds for a new appeal. At the age of 19 most people have not yet fully lived. For William this fact is true. Not being able to experience growing pains in the real-world, William has been forced to grow up mentally in prison. I try my best to keep his spirits high by communicating daily with him and by visiting him. Lately I haven't been able to visit him because of covid & the restrictions in the prison. The changes were very upsetting to both of us, however through this book William's voice can still be heard.

William was a kid that was easily influenced by the street culture. Hearing the stories from drug dealers seemed more like adventures to him. Most kids want unlimited amounts of fun over responsibilities but what they don't understand is all good things come to an end. The street culture usually ends in death or jail. Very rarely do we see success stories from people who live by the street code. For most things in life, you can normally say that a person has a 50/50 chance of succeeding but in the streets it's not a 50/50 chance, more like 10 percent. Honestly the odds probably are lower than that when I think about it. What things or people are influencing your choices? Is that influence guiding you in a positive or negative direction?

While we are on the topic lets touch on success. What does success mean to you? Really think about it for a second. People risk their freedom every day for designer clothes, foreign or sport cars, expensive jewelry, & popularity. Is that success? Material gains are not success because those are things that can be easily taken away. Success to me is finding your purpose in life, finding your soulmate, creating a family, taking care of your responsibilities, starting a business or working a job that makes you happy, inspiring & motivating others to be great, creating generational wealth, & finding peace within yourself to name a few. Temporary success often blinds people who have yet to feel the pain that comes with instant gratification. Longevity means everything. "The game is chess not checkers" a phrase I heard often growing up in the streets of Detroit. It's a thinking man's game but when that pressure is on and your world is crumbling down around you, was it really worth the consequences? Don't let instant gratification blind you. Don't let temporary gains stop you from creating generational wealth.

William expressed how he wished his father had more of a positive influence on him when he was a child and how he wanted a deeper connection with his mother. Like many people that may be reading this book, William's father was in and out of prison while he was growing up. His didn't set a good example for William. The saying "The apple doesn't fall far from the tree" is often true when it comes to "THE CYCLE". The Cycle I'm referring to is the revolving door of jails and prisons for so many families in urban communities around the world. I often hear people being excited about being the first person in their family to go to college or graduate college. I remember having a friend who was so excited

15

about being the first person in his family to graduate high school. Breaking "The Cycle" comes in all forms especially with men with their kids. So many fatherless sons and daughters growing up in a world looking for love in all the wrong places because they are missing the love from the man that birthed them. Let's break that cycle collectively.

I often think back to those nights when I was in Sheridan Correctional Facility sleeping on the top bunk watching the news frowning at the number of deaths they would have in a day or a weekend. The same thing I was thinking then is what I'm thinking at this exact moment, "WHY ARE YOUNG PEOPLE SO VIOLENT AND SO ANGRY?" This question is for the world. I recently talked to my family member in Omaha, NE and we had a brief conversation about a young man who got gunned down inside of a mall. Why are we so eager to throw our lives away? I pray for the day in the urban communities when teenagers don't have to grow up ready and willing to commit violent acts. Society plays a big part in the corruption of the mind. Often, in certain neighborhoods, fear supersedes love because of the fear of violence. To be feared is a sense of power that leads to destruction if used by the wrong person. Growing up, my brothers and I were influenced by drug dealers, hit men, and pimps. I'm 36 and not one person from the streets that influenced me as a kid is doing anything productive with their life today. Most are dead or in prison and the few that our free are barely surviving.

In one of many of our discussions, William, believes that people resort to the streets to make money because chasing the American dream takes a lifetime to accomplish. For that reason, people rather risk their freedom than to work a job. William, like many others growing up around the world, neglected the counsel from his parents and other authority figures. A decision that he truly regrets but expresses that at the time "distractions were more fun than lessons."

1 Corinthians 13:11
"When I was a child, I spoke like a child,
I thought like a child, I reasoned like a child.
When I became a man, I gave up childish ways."

Only a fool despises wisdom. There is a time in everyone's life when they are lost or make questionable decisions. Before a person finds themself, they burn bridges and hurt the people that love them the most. It was a time in my life when I didn't talk to anyone in my family. I was so stubborn and lost mentally. The best thing that happened to me was that I realized I needed to be a better person. In order for me to grow in every aspect of life I needed to be a better person not only to other people but also to myself. If you are reading this and have ignored wise counsel from people in your life how long will you continue? Will it take you going to prison to change? Will it take you to almost lose your life before you wake up?

Addicted

I'm worth more than the curse I've inherited at birth
I share Mother Earth soil like skin
I breathe the breeze of my existence
Digest poisons some cured
Addicted I am
I am and yet I'm not
A bad role model
Mentally ignorant without a plan
Son of a man
God's image, imagine me filthy rich still needing a friend
Through sin I explain myself
Right or wrong good choices are bittersweet
Non credible but incredible
Expect more
I expect nothing more than disappointment from my peers
Because what appears to be is not
I am not your everyday cup of tea
No one plays cricket where I'm from
You won't even hear one
The hottest summers give me the chills
Cold sweats, fear no man, but nervous I am
Capable of anything everything at my grasp
My whole life, you don't know the half
Of me imitating iconic individuals
Influential, Addicted I am
-poem written by William Moseley Jr.

Chapter 3: Karma

"Karma has no menu.
You get served
what you deserve."
-Unknown

Karma is a word that we often hear and use. However, do we actually understand the meaning of karma? Good or bad you will reap what you sow. If one studies efficiently for an upcoming test, I presume that person will receive good karma by passing with a good grade. On the other hand, if one cheats on a test one day that person will get caught and receive bad karma and their word will always be questioned.

If a track star takes illegal drugs to enhance their performance, that person will be disqualified and banned. If a person uses drugs their karma could be that they will either die from using drugs or their children may also pick up the habit. If a person lives a gangster lifestyle and kills people, one day that person's karma will be that they will get killed or someone close to them may be harmed in retaliation.

Karma doesn't always come back like a person may think. When I was a teenager, a lot of people I knew died due to gun violence. However, two murders stand out to me because they were my friends, and they were so young. Chris died inside of a crack house. He was only 14 years old selling drugs for a dealer on the East side of Detroit. Chris was shot and killed by a drug addict who robbed the drug house and was later caught by the police. Chris's mother was devastated that she lost her son. My other friend Antonio was murdered in Omaha, NE at the age of 13. He was gunned down standing outside of Pleasantview Housing Projects. Antonio could have been a stellar athlete, however, the negative influences of his environment led him to an early grave. Both Chris and Antonio are dearly missed by their family and friends.

When I think about Chris and Antonio, one thing seems to be in common with other youth who leave this earth to an untimely death. Both Chris and Antonio had a lot of freedom at an early age to make decisions for themselves. It seems like in this world we live in it harder and harder for single mothers to raise their kids. Even during co-parenting sometimes, it can be a struggle to get a kid structured if the parents aren't on the same page. Due to social media and the changes with technology these kids are growing up faster as each day passes. I can't imagine being a parent that has lost their child. My heart goes out to you if you are reading this and have lost a child in anyway, especially to violence. I believe to bury your child is every parent's worst nightmare. Having to do so, however, must bring up so many regrets. So many thoughts of ways that the parent could have done things differently. In some aspects parents struggle with being too strict and not strict enough. Being a friend and not a parent is one thing I notice more and more when I see people with kids these days.

As parents we must protect our children at all costs from this cruel and unsafe world. We must monitor what our kids are watching on television and who they are talking to because kids are heavily influenced by things they see and people they talk to. We have to spend time with our kids and allow them to express themselves without feeling ashamed. We must fill our kids with so much self-esteem & confidence that they aren't scared to fail. We must instill in our kids the proper morals and values so that they won't be misled.

I come across many adults who still hold resentment towards their parents or care givers for not leading them in the right direction or for giving up on them. One of the main reasons in my eyes kids get led the wrong way by their parents is because there are so many teenagers having children, and they end up growing up together. Another reason kids get led the wrong way or neglected by their parents is because of jealousy. It sounds crazy right; you would think that a parent would want their child's life to be better than theirs, but some people are jealous of their kids. An example would be a woman neglecting and being abusive to her daughter because she is more beautiful. Another example would be a single mother neglecting her son or treating him differently than her other kids because the kid reminds her of his father who left her for another woman. The most common example is a boy growing up without the guidance of his father because of incarceration or the father is immature and not fully ready to take care of his responsibilities like a man. I'll never understand how a man can make a baby with a woman but leave his son or daughter fatherless. Neglect is traumatizing when you crave love. Growing up I had friends whose parents were crack heads. I can't even imagine what that felt like because my mom never used drugs. The impact it had on their lives took a turn for the worse at a young age. It's imperative that we pay attention to the things we expose kids to because corrupting the mind before the proper understanding is established can be very dangerous. We are creatures of habit. What shouldn't be normal is normal to some. Hunger, poverty, lack of clothing, manipulation, neglect, verbal abuse, physical abuse, and molestation are only a few issues that people become accustomed to dealing with.

Discipline and correction are imperative for a child to grow and develop properly. Prisons are full of people who make careless decisions. Decisions where the consequence is time away from family, friends, children, money, and other responsibilities. Growing up it seemed like prison was a part of becoming a man. That couldn't be farther from the truth. When I was a kid, every man in my neighborhood had been to prison. When I asked about someone I hadn't seen for a long time, they were either in prison or dead. For some people the answers are still the same today. The world has us so blind and corrupted, damaging our future before we even have a chance. So ready to take a life, to commit murder, to harm others. So ready to take another person's possessions. If we fail to discipline and correct our kids, they will never understand that there are consequences for bad behavior.

Chapter 4: Be a better friend to yourself

"You are your own best friend
And worst enemy;
Only you can take yourself higher
Or make yourself fall even lower."
-Dr. Prem Jagyasi

Something I struggled with growing up was my decision making. I would put other people before myself. People who I thought were cool, people I wanted respect from, people who seemed like they had life figured out, etc. I didn't understand the true meaning of, "Be a better friend to Yourself", until I was sitting in a prison cell just shortly after I recovered from getting shot and almost losing my life. That was the wakeup call I needed. The reality check that put everything in perspective. I sat and thought about every time I could have died or been harmed by not really caring about myself. If I really cared about myself like I should, then I wouldn't have almost lost my life to gun violence and I wouldn't have been committing crimes which led me to give 4 years to the penal system.

Truth is we as people know right from wrong, we just choose to live life on the edge. We know that red meat and pork aren't good for the body & can be cancerous, however, people still eat steak and pork chops. The question is why? Why is it so hard for us to be our own best friend? Why is it so hard for us to treat our bodies with respect and not use drugs? Why is it so hard for us to use protection when we have sex so we don't have kids that we aren't going to take care of? Why is it so hard for us to end toxic relationships? Why is it so hard for us to tell people no when they ask for something? Why is it so hard for us to own up to our mistakes and challenge ourselves to do better? Why is it so hard for us to focus and get to the next level? If you also struggle with any of these situations, take some time to assess why you struggle and how you can change. It really boils down to self-love.

One of my close friends, Danny Ray Robinson Jr., is doing a natural life prison sentence in Lincoln, NE for murder. He was convicted because of statements from people he once called his friends. One of Danny's flaws, like many of us, was that he liked to impress people and he took on other people's problems. Every city I've ever been to has its own gang culture or street culture but one thing that remains the same is the mentality of the people who are raised in these communities. The streets have a way of brain washing people into thinking that the gangster & the hustler lifestyle comes with longevity. Truthfully, the gangster and hustler lifestyle are adventurous and exciting, however, it is short lived for most. What I mean by short lived is that most people who live this lifestyle are either dead or in jail before the age of 25. The law says that youth between the ages of 18-24 will be charged as adults if they commit crimes. However, scientific studies show that the brain is still developing through early 20's of a person's life. Still a judge will sentence an 18-year-old to life in prison without the chance of parole. Could you imagine being that 18-year-old living life like it's a video game, living life recklessly like actions don't have consequences, and then being sentenced to life in prison with no parole? Most 18-year-old don't understand how serious that is until they wake up in their cell at 25, then they wake up in their cell at 30, appeals get denied, then they wake up in their cell at 40 and then 50 etc. People grow up in prison and their minds change for the better, however their consequence is to be immobilized by prison gates and their lack of resources to the outside world. People in this situation often blame their parents or other people for their decision making or their mistakes. Instead of looking in the mirror and owning their choices they hold resentment and anger towards people who may have played a parental role in their life. Until a person can look in the mirror and own up to their mistakes and decisions that person will never grow mentally.

Danny was sentenced to life without parole at the age of 25. His case leaves questions if the statements from the witnesses (his former friends) are even credible because they only snitched to get sentence reduction for drug cases. It's a dirty game. Danny got picked up in 2004 and it is now 2022 and he is still fighting for his freedom. Although 20 years has almost gone by, he is still optimistic that one day he will be released and reunited with his family. Like many people who may be reading this book, Danny Ray Robinson Jr. was also introduced to the streets at an early age. He said he was pressured by family members and his peers to be like his father and his uncles who were gangsters, pimps, and hustlers. Danny believes that if he had better role models, he could have gone a different route. "Being poor doesn't come with many opportunities, it only leaves you hopeless." Danny explained that he was introduced to violence at an early age and when you think about it, most people are introduced to violence at an early age considering when kids are disciplined by their parents. When I was kid, we got spankings with belts and branches off bushes that were called switches. Danny's theory is by being physically disciplined as a kid we began to believe that whenever we are upset, we can physically assault the people who have wronged us. Not to mention that same behavior is perpetuated in our music and in the movies we watch. So, most people are being raised by what they see if they don't have good influences in their lives.

Danny prides himself these days on helping younger inmates who are incarcerated in his facility to develop their mind, so they won't keep making the same decisions. He expresses that most criminals don't have any special talents, therefore selling drugs gives people an advantage over those that are already privileged. A lot of people fall victim to the streets because of the notoriety and popularity that comes with making money, which leaves people to believe their doing nothing wrong. Most youth who turn to the streets have learning disorders which causes them to fail in school and believe they aren't smart enough to excel in education. It's so important for kids to have parents who are invested in them. Without the proper support almost every kid will take shortcuts and begin to question themselves. Danny states that nobody wants to look stupid or admit that they learn slower than other students, therefore most kids just stay quiet and drop out. Danny admits to struggling in school with ADHD and later dropping out because he had no support. He states that for kids growing up in the ghetto it's hard to see the importance of school because the only successful people that we see are drug dealers, gang bangers, pimps, or athletes. Through all of his hardships Danny now understands why school is a steppingstone to a better life which requires discipline.

I asked Danny if you could send a message around the world to kids everywhere what would you say? "I would tell them that you can be whatever you want to be. Even though you can't see it just look inside of yourself. If you work hard enough and smart enough, one day you will figure it out. Trying to impress people and gang banging only limits your chances on finding true peace. There is small room for error because of who you are and where you are starting from. Stay focused!"

Danny wakes up every day full of regret. He left so much on the table, so much unreached potential due to bad decisions. How does a person get used to life in prison? It sounds impossible. He states "that he is still being held accountable for the actions of a person he has grown out of. In his new life with his new mindset, he has so much purpose, so much to offer but nowhere to flourish or offer it to. Danny admits that when he was free, he was unforgiving, selfish, vengeful, deceitful, violent and disrespectful to everyone. Currently in his life, he is the opposite of all of those things. Prison has given him time to grow and reflect on the person he was and change into the person he should have been all along. Danny explains that at one point he was full of hate and now he is full of love. "I have forgiven my enemies even when they didn't ask for it. I no longer look to violence to resolve a problem. Being that I'm in prison violence is only used for self-defense or when I have no other option. I have natural life in prison, there is no reason to lie about anything and I no longer disrespect people or myself." The last time we spoke Danny talked about how hopeless he used to be and how he dreams even in the daytime now.

All the mental toughness and power that he has in his mind only to be trapped behind bars is mind boggling. Writing this book makes me think more about all the other men who are in his shoes and all the young men who are potential candidates for the same future. This is not the life that was made for us. Waking up every day in a prison cell is not a bad dream it's a nightmare. It takes a different type of person to stay positive under these circumstances and Danny Ray Robinson Jr. is a soldier. Danny acknowledges that his perception of success was wrong on so many levels. "Success to me used to be how many people I beat up or shot, how much money I made in one day selling drugs, buying all the cars & clothes I could ever desire, and how many girls I had sex with in one day. Now I find success in creating opportunities for my people, so they won't have to go through what I had to go through. Every day I work towards becoming the best version of myself so the people who look up to me can see the positive things I'm accomplishing instead of the negative things I used to glorify."

Chapter 5: Growing up in Prison

**"The cruelest prison of all
is the prison of the mind"
-Piri Thomas**

Believe it or not you can't avoid maturity. You can prolong it, but you can't avoid it. Eventually people understand that they must abide by certain laws and respect people. Either you can figure this out on your own or the penal system will help you out. When we go to prison all we are doing is enslaving ourselves and humiliating ourselves. I've been to prison. I've walked in shackles. I've taken years of freedom away from my life. I share the same pain as many people who may be reading this. We all have different struggles throughout life, but we can't let adversity defeat us. If we don't find a way to discipline ourselves most of us will spend more time locked up, then we spend free. Slavery is over but modern-day slavery is incarceration. Do you want to be free, or do you want to be a slave? Before you make a reckless decision think about if you want to be free or if you want to be a slave!

The older I get the more I realize how much time I've wasted living a life that wasn't for me. Time is precious but your freedom is everything. Without freedom time means nothing. If you are reading this and you are incarcerated, or you will be incarcerated soon please take your time seriously. They can trap the body, but they can't trap the mind. Be productive with your time please. Prison is said to be made to deter people from crime but that is far from truth. Prison is designed to cage us like animals. Are you an animal? You get told when you can eat and when you can take a shower. You get told when you can come out of your cell and when you can see your loved ones, that's if you have any left that are able to visit you. Something I learned from my prison bid was that if I govern myself, no authority will have anything to say to me.

I want to introduce you to someone who is like a little brother to me. Deshawn Jones is another person I'm in consistent communication with through letters. He and my brother William were close friends growing up, so I always looked at him like another brother. Literally watched them learn lessons in the streets & have to deal with their consequences and grow up mentally in prison. Your past affects your future. The sooner a

35

person gets started on taking life serious on a positive note, the sooner that person will find peace and success.

Deshawn is incarcerated in the Michigan Department of Corrections for Second Degree Murder. He took a plea deal where he was sentenced 23-45 years, his earliest release date is 2036. After being locked up for 8 years his mindset has changed and he sees a lot of things from a different perspective. Deshawn makes it very clear that he didn't have any adults in his life that could educate him not to adopt the street lifestyle. Deshawn grew up in a crack house and his parents and older siblings were drug dealers. The street lifestyle was the only agenda. No business talks or school talks. Being a product of his environment caused him to be influenced by his peers because they all came from broken homes. Kids from broken homes usually join gangs or start gangs to develop a sense of family. In the past Deshawn had a lot of issues because of his gang involvement. In prison gang members are targeted by authority figures just as much as they are on the streets. Deshawn has lost privileges & has been sent to high level institutions because of his gang participation. His gang involvement has caused him more problems than it has helped him throughout his life. Being a part of a gang can pull a person into disciplinary actions even if that person had nothing to do with the crimes the gang is being accused of.

Two famous rappers, Young Thug and Gunna, have been indicted among 26 other members of their YSL record label under the Rico Act for drugs and murders. I'm almost certain that all 28 people in that indictment didn't commit the crimes they are accused of but just because of their affiliation to a criminal organization they will be charged for conspiracy. A lot of people turn into snitches because they join gangs not knowing what they are actually signing up for. Are you prepared to spend life in prison for something that you didn't do? That's a question you need to ask yourself before you join a gang. If you are in a gang, how are you helping your community? Because if you are not building your community up then you are tearing it down. What affect will that have on the generations to come?

Deshawn once told me that if he could change anything about his childhood, he would have finished school and pursued a legitimate career. I still haven't figured out why people would rather be broke than to get a job and have some consistent cash flow. Why is having a job lame? If you don't want to work for anybody then why not start a business? If you can run a successful drug operation, then you can run a Fortune 500 company. You don't have to look over your shoulder when you are living right. Karma seems to have a funny way of showing up when we least expect it. A 9-5 doesn't seem like enough money to take care of responsibilities and provide for a household but how can you provide for a household in prison? How can you raise your kids from prison?

Deshawn blames sex, drugs, money, and popularity as the reasons why kids become distracted and lose focus on their education. Not having the proper role models to advise kids on the power and importance of education is the reason many fall short. Even still, kids that grow up in 2 parent homes fall victim to the streets and commit crimes. A study done in 1998 in the U.S. tracked over 6,400 boys for more than 20 years and found that children who grow up without their biological father are three times more likely to commit crimes that lead to incarceration than children who come from unbroken families. (Harper & McLanahan, 1998). 70% of incarcerated adults come from single-parent families and boys who are raised without their father present are twice as likely to end up in jail. (Georgia Supreme Court

Commission on Children, Marriage and Family Law, 2004). When only one parent is in the home, it's often more difficult to supervise all of a kid's interactions. The lack of children having parental supervision and the proper role models is what leads to juveniles increasing the use of drugs, criminal activity and delinquency.

Deshawn explains that his days now consist of strengthening his mind by reading books dealing with entrepreneurship and education. "Even though I'm incarcerated life for me is evolution. I strive to surround myself around like-minded individuals that challenge me. I also strive to be a better provider and a family-oriented man. The best advice I can give to kids is to find a mentor that can give them constructive advice & guidance on how to become whatever they desire to be in life." Dame Dash, Master P, and Steve Harvey are three people who I consider to be my mentors and I have no personal relationship with them, nor have I ever met Dame Dash or Master P. You don't have to know a person or meet a person for them to be your mentor. If you are reading this and you lack the proper guidance or influence, it may be time to think outside of the box. Find a mentor that can help you grow and learn from them. In my spare time all I do is watch Dame Dash, Master P, and Steve Harvey interviews because they have accomplished goals in their life that one day I hope to achieve as well. No matter your circumstance, you owe it to yourself to give your best effort to elevate yourself in life. The world is a beautiful place, too beautiful to spend it confined in a cell.

Personal connections are important to Deshawn, especially after losing his mother. "Our relationship was the best relationship I've ever had with a person. She was the best mother I could ask for". His morals and values have changed considerably. It's so easy for a person to give up mentally in his circumstances. Giving up is always the easiest route but nothing worth having comes easy. The fight for freedom and peace is worth every sacrifice.

"I value life itself more and I don't take anything for granted. I value and worship the Creator. I value my loved ones, friends and family. I morally seek discipline and I always conduct myself with respect." Eight years ago, Deshawn's conversation and demeanor was different. He lived his life on the edge and like most teenagers committing crimes, Deshawn didn't understand how much he was damaging his future. Although your past can affect your future don't let your past dictate who you are.

The world needs more positive leaders that don't have hidden agendas. A voice for the people who are too afraid to be uncomfortable and be different. Deshawn believes that his strength to become a better person comes from the Creator. "I believe in a Higher Power/God and I believe that the devil is real. I believe it's insight in every religion but I follow no religion. Religion is just something that divides us. I believe in an original creator of all things." His perspective is not farfetched. Understanding and acknowledging that there is a higher power is a major step in the right direction. In order for a troubled person to maintain the proper focus one must have faith in not only themselves but in a power greater than themselves. Not everyone is open to talks about God or religion. It takes maturity and open mindedness to engage in such discussions, but such discussions are really needed in the development of our hearts.

Chapter 6: Living in your purpose

"There is no greater gift
You can give or receive
Than to honor your calling.
It's why you were born.
And how you become
most truly alive."
-Oprah Winfrey

There's a voice inside of your head that you have been avoiding. There's a feeling inside your soul that you have been neglecting. There's wisdom from other people that you haven't opened your mind to. How much time will go by before you wake up? How many losses will you take before you are ready for a change? It's 24 hours in a day, how many of those hours do you spend chasing your dreams? How many of those hours do you spend living in your purpose? One of the problems with us is that we spend more time living someone else's dream than we do living our own. We spend more time celebrating the success of others more than we celebrate our own. We set an alarm to make sure we wake up on time to go to work or school, we leave notification for important things that we don't want to forget. But what about our FOCUS? What are we doing to make sure that we are staying focused and what are we doing to get back focused once we get sidetracked? Do you have the right people in your circle? Meaning if you are going in the right direction, you must cut ties with people who are going in the wrong direction. If you're plan is to elevate in life, then you must be around like-minded people. So many people have the crab in the bucket mentality and don't realize it. You must separate yourself from people who will pull you back down to the place that you are trying to make it out from.

I just left Los Angeles last week, 5/1/22, for the 30-year anniversary of the 1992 Gang Truce Peace Treaty between different Crip & Blood gangs on the east side of L.A. It was inspirational and motivational to be around so many people who want peace in not only their community but also the world. Growing up in the gang culture I understand that so many people fall victim to the streets. So many people die before they get old. So many teenagers get locked up and charged as an adult because of their crimes. Every day we are killing the future Martin Luther King's & Malcom X's. Everyday a mother loses her son. Everyday a little boy or girl loses their father. The world is so full of hate. The world uses religion & gangs to separate us and cause confusion. In reality, we all should be one; unified. One race, the human race!

Nipsey Hussle is someone I admire because he understood how important it is to motivate and inspire other people to believe in themselves and to chase their dreams. He literally came from nothing and turned himself into a legend. Nipsey went from gang banging to being nominated for a Grammy, owning businesses and also a community activist who touched the hearts of many around the world. That can be you, no matter what age you are or what you have done there's still time for you to leave your mark in a positive meaningful way in the world & be remembered forever.

If today was your last day to live and you had a chance to write yourself a letter of regrets and apologize to yourself, what would it say? We blame so much on other things and people, but our worse enemy is our ignorance. We ignore the fact that we only get one life. One life to experience true happiness and peace. One life to take advantage of the relationships we have with friends and family members. One life to live in our purpose and create a legacy that last longer than our life span. One life to live as long as we can and accomplish as much as we can.

The world is changing right before our eyes are you paying attention? Fentanyl overdose deaths are at an all-time high in the United States. Drill music has made it normal for rappers to slander the names of dead people in their songs. Several states have banned Abortion and Planned B pills taking the rights away from women who may have been molested or raped. The police are using social media to indict people and charge them with crimes. People are more worried about proving they are "real" to the same people who talk about them when the police are kicking in their door. These days it seems like it's more people that are part of the problem than the solution.

Many people become discouraged easily. People will have a vision or a dream but not the will power and the patience to see it through. Nothing comes easy and nothing worth having is free. Every bump in the road will one day become a smooth surface with construction. Change is constant. Everyday work on your weaknesses so that one day they will become your strengths. Never live in the past. Learn from your mistakes but don't dwell on them. When I played basketball in high school I used to get upset after I made a mistake or a bad possession because I wanted to have the perfect game. Coach Cannon used to tell me to let it go and clear my mind and focus on the next play because I can't change what's already happened. Life is similar to basketball in a sense, although mistakes in basketball can be worked out, some mistakes in life are forever. Your future can be changed drastically by one decision. Think outside of the box. Dare to be different. Some people don't want anything out of life but material things. They want the nicest jewelry, cars, clothes, things that hold no real value. Be someone of substance, someone with meaning. Wealthy people pour wealth into other people. Imagine becoming successful and instilling the same morals and values you have into other people. Imagine the success stories and the people who will uplift your name because you were the person in their life that helped them grow. The person that helped them believe they had a purpose and that God had a plan for their life. Never underestimate the plans The Creator of the world has for your life.

Each year it's imperative to grow mentally and not be in the same place that you were last year. "Slow motion, is better than no motion". If you lay a brick everyday soon you will have a brick wall. A focused person sets themselves apart from those who lack discipline. Most people desire to be great but don't understand that it comes with much sacrifice. Hard work beats talent when talent doesn't work. It's not always about who's the most talented, sometimes it's about who's hungrier. Currently in your life what's more important than your focus? If you have people in your life who take you away from focusing on your goals and passions, then you need to dismiss them out of your life. Sometimes we choose the wrong people to be in our life. The interchanging of energy is very important, and you should be very careful who you let in your immediate circle. Some people can give you a positive energy that is unmatched and some people can drain your energy away because of their personal problems. Energy is contagious. Give your energy to people who believe in you and who want to see you do well in life.

While incarcerated in Illinois Department of Correction at Sheridan Correctional Facility from 2013-2015, I was involved in a program that is designed to reduce recidivism, gang prevention, and drug use. Every inmate that successfully completed the program got credited good time and was granted to be released from prison 6 months to a year earlier than their scheduled date. As I progressed through the program, I met Benny Lee who was one of the counselors assigned to my building. Benny Lee was a former leader of the Conservative Vice Lords. In 1979 he and 15 other people were indicted on 15 counts of murder, 2 counts of attempted murder, and mob action after a riot broke out and 3 guards were killed along with other inmates. For 3 years Benny was on death row until he was acquitted and he now works as a counselor through Illinois Department of Corrections as well as other gang prevention programs in Chicago. Benny dedicates his life to help people who are struggling to find the confidence inside of themselves to change. He explained to us that everyone will not understand your want for change but that the change is not for everyone, the change is for you. While making positive changes in his life he ran into some opposition from members of the Vice Lord Nation and eventually decided that it was best he dropped his flag in order to continue his new journey. Seeing Benny talk to us with such compassion opened my eyes. A man that once had so much power in the gang world left it all for peace, for a future. The question is how important is your future to you? We have free will to choose the life we want to live but most of us only get one chance. While some of us get chance after chance and still fail to change the structure of our life and environment. Benny taught me that when God blesses you with a second chance at life, a second chance at freedom, you have been chosen to save lives by helping people find their true purpose. Your purpose is not to get killed gang banging. Your purpose is not to spend your life in prison. Your purpose is not to leave your children without a parent. Your purpose is not to be a drug addict.

I mentioned earlier that I went to Los Angeles, California to attend the 30-year Anniversary of the 1992 gang truce peace treaty between the Crips and Bloods. I was astonished to see Mayor Eric Garcetti, councilmen, the community, crip gang members, blood gang members, Latino gang members and police attending this event fighting for peace. Charles "Q-Bone" Rachal is one of the faces and voices of the 1992 peace treaty. For the past 30 years he and many others have been dedicated to turning their lives around from active gang members to peace makers in not only their community but throughout Los Angeles as well. Q-Bone and the other members of the

30-year peace treaty all received plaques from the city of L.A. for their continuous obligation and their help to end gang violence. Their efforts encouraged me so much to be a part of the solution and not the problem. I grew up in the gang culture, so I understand the mindset of the average gang member. However, to see hundreds of gang members in one place for 6 hours without quarrel was truly amazing because even the active gang members are open to the idea of changing the course of history. It's a struggle to transform hate to love. Pastor Shep Crawford and Minister Tony Muhammad both shared the stage expressing the message of love no matter your religion. Pastor Shep Crawford is the founder and pastor of The Experience Christian Ministries in Los Angeles, California. While Tony Muhammad, also known as Abdul Malik Sayyid Muhammad, is the regional representative for Nation of Islam on the West Coast. Christians do not hate Muslims and Muslims do not hate Christians. They both explained that there is a misconception and that the world needs to be told the truth. Just like communities use gangs to separate people and cause conflict, without the proper knowledge the world does the same with religion.

Life is a marathon don't rush. Find yourself, love yourself, believe in yourself. Don't settle for a life that you aren't satisfied with. Be creative and think outside of the box. If staying focused was easy, then everyone would do it. Focus is not easy, but it is mandatory if you want to be successful. There is a light inside of you but the darkness inside of you may be covering it up. It's time to get rid of that darkness. It's time to show everyone all the good things you are capable of. God didn't create you to be incarcerated, God created you to prosper. January 1, 2022, I opened a clothing store for my brand "Izani Collection". I'm so far out of my comfort zone as I try to make up for lost time when I wasn't committed to being the best version of myself. Every day I learn new things and sometimes I become discouraged when business is not going the way I would like. However, I'm closer to my destination than where I started from. With everything we do we must have patience for our dreams to blossom. Uplifting and stimulating the minds of others brings me much joy. That is my purpose to lead by example and help others reach their potential. What's your purpose? It's definitely not to steer kids in the wrong direction or to commit crimes giving your life to the penal system. In this world it's easier to have a negative outlook than it is to have a positive outlook because the world will broadcast bad things faster than they will broadcast good things. The lesson is not be so impressionable that you trade your freedom for material things or instant gratification. If you are 16 years or younger reading this book, please think before you act because when you turn 17 you can be charged as an adult for a crime and potentially end up going to prison. Understand that tough guys either get killed before they grow old or spend their life in prison wishing they can have another chance. Understand that once you start burning bridges they can never be crossed again.

My heart goes out to the youth all over the world because I know firsthand how it feels to be lost and not know it. If you are 17 years or older reading this book and you have been incarcerated or have wasted time living a life that's not for you, what are you going to do about it? Are you going to continue to make the same decisions hoping that something different will come from it? I sure hope not. I hope you will wake up before it's too late. I hope you will look in the mirror and re-invent yourself to the best version you can possibly be.

The sky is the limit. The most dangerous person is a focused person. Get determined and stay determined. Eliminate anything in your life that takes your peace and your focus away. I'm not perfect, I'm just like you. We may be a different race, believe in a different religion, we may be a different gender, we may come from a different upbringing but understand we all face adverse situations. We all need to find our purpose and stay true to our fate. Everyday you wake up, should be lived with no regrets. Peace & Blessings!

Silence

Speechless thoughts speak volumes
outside my meditative state
Awkward silence becomes beautiful
& Timeless when my mind just naps
While I'm trapped still awake
Hear no evil
See no evil
Speak no evil
Experiencing inner peace
To warm for the cold hearted
Alone again
I never known a friend to befriend threw silence
Have you?
Have you ever set in silence?
Silenced by arguments in your head
You can't even get a word in
Convinced, I'm convinced I never experienced silence
My mind just won't stop learning
Chiming in or guiding me threw life's obstacles
I suppose as time goes on, I'll experience silence
Hear that
Sounds like another personal problem
Problem is I'm more comfortable around sound than silence
-poem written by William Moseley Jr.

Georgia Supreme Court Commission on
Children, Marriage, and Family Law(2004).
Strategic Plan citing Cynthia C. Harper and
Sara S. McLanahan. "Father Absence and
Youth Incarceration," Journal of Research on
Adolescence 14, no. 3: 369-397

Harper, C. & McLanahan, S. S., "Father
Absence and youth incarceration, "findings
Presented at the 1998 meeting of the American
Sociological Association, San Francisco, CA.

William Mosley MDOC(739875)

Deshawn Jones MDOC(728405)

Danny Robinson NDOC(61657)